DATE DUE

MAR

HOLOCAUST BIOGRAPHIES

Albert Speer
Hitler's Architect

Fred Ramen

THE ROSEN PUBLISHING GROUP, INC.
NEW YORK

Published in 2001 by The Rosen Publishing Group, Inc.
29 East 21st Street, New York, NY 10010

First Edition

Library of Congress Cataloging-in-Publication Data

Ramen, Fred.
Albert Speer : Hitler's architect / by Fred Ramen.
p. cm. — (Holocaust biographies)
Includes bibliographical references and index.
ISBN 0-8239-3372-5
1. Speer, Albert, 1905—Juvenile literature. 2. Nazis—
Biography—Juvenile literature. 3. Germany—History—1933-
1945—Juvenile literature. I. Title. II. Series.
DD247.S63 R36 2001
943.086'092—dc21

                                              2001001849

Manufactured in the United States of America

Contents

■ Forced Labor Camps　　● Extermination Camps

This map shows the location of some of the Nazi labor camps, where inmates were forced to work as slave laborers.

Introduction

During the morning of October 17, 1946, several prisoners of war were ordered by their Allied captors to clean out a number of prison cells in Nuremberg, Germany. This beautiful city had been the home of the Nazi Party before and during World War II (1939–1945) and the place where Nazi leader Adolf Hitler conducted many famous rallies. Then it was home to the International Tribunal of War Crimes, a court set up by the victorious Allied powers after the war. The tribunal's mission was a first in world history: It would put the former leaders of Nazi Germany on trial for "crimes against humanity."

The cells being cleaned had been occupied by Nazi leaders who had been convicted and sentenced to death by the tribunal. Before dawn that day, ten of the men had been hanged; one, former Reich Marshall Hermann Göring, had cheated his captors by committing suicide. As a final humiliation, and a reminder of what might have befallen them, three of the prisoners were later ordered to clean up the gymnasium where the hangings took place. One of these prisoners was Albert Speer, Hitler's favorite architect and former minister of production for all of Germany, who had escaped the hangman by admitting his—and Germany's—guilt during his trial. Although he had spared his own life by taking responsibility for Nazi atrocities, Speer would remain a controversial figure even after his death.

1. Early Life

Perhaps more than any other man, Albert Speer was responsible for allowing Germany to prolong World War II. His management of industrial production and the economy kept the German armed forces fighting even as the country's factories and cities were being disabled by the Allied air force. How, then, was Albert Speer one of only a few top German leaders to avoid the death sentence for the crimes of the Nazi government? He was released from prison in 1966, and many people questioned just how much he had repented for the sins of the Nazis—and also how many of those crimes he had committed himself without ever admitting to them.

An Unhappy Childhood

Berthold Konrad Hermann Albert Speer was born on March 19, 1905, in Mannheim, a prosperous city in southern Germany. He was the second of three sons born to Albert Friedrich and Mathilde Speer. Both Speer's father and grandfather were architects. His father had established a comfortable living as a practicing architect when he married Speer's mother, the daughter of a wealthy industrial family. This made the Speers much better off than most Germans, if not exactly rich.

Although the Speer family had a large apartment in Mannheim, they preferred to live in a house built by Albert's father near the town of Heidelberg, which is famous for its world-class university. Speer hated the Heidelberg house, associating it with memories of a loveless childhood.

His parents' marriage was not a happy one. Speer's father was cold and distant and Speer's mother was more concerned with the family's social status than with her children. As was typical for middle- and upper-class children of the day, young Albert was raised by servants, particularly by a French governess, Mademoiselle Blum. (Strangely enough, considering the direction Speer's life would take later, his governess was Jewish.) However, when Albert was nine, Mademoiselle Blum left the country because war had broken out between Germany and France.

This war was World War I (1914–1919), which up to that point was the worst war in history to be fought in Europe, and the first truly global conflict. World War I was the most influential event in the twentieth century in Europe; its results directly contributed to the fighting of a second, even more terrible, world war. To understand Speer's life, first we must examine the Germany that Albert Speer was born into, and why it ended up in a worldwide conflict with the other nations of Europe.

Germany's History

Unlike France and Britain, Germany didn't become a unified nation until relatively late, in 1871. Before that, various small German states had existed independently of one another. Gradually, however, one of these independent states, Prussia, came to dominate the rest of Germany, winning a series of wars with the other European powers that established the Prussian (and later German) reputation for military efficiency. The last of these wars, the Franco-Prussian War (1870–1871), fought by France against Prussia and its allies among the other German states, ended in a humiliating defeat for the French and the creation of a unified German empire under the king of Prussia, Wilhelm I.

As part of the treaty that ended the war, the French had to give Germany the province of Alsace-Lorraine, a portion of France with a mixed German and French population. This

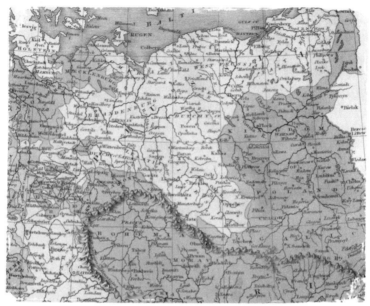

Before Germany became a unified nation in 1871, several small, independent German states existed.

infuriated French nationalists and made France a permanent enemy of Germany, even to the point of forming an alliance with their centuries-old rival, England. The major countries of Europe—France, Britain, Germany, and Russia—found themselves more often in conflict, and they continued to build up their armed forces, waiting for the inevitable spark that would set off war in Europe.

When the spark—the assassination of the heir to the throne of the Austro-Hungarian Empire, one of Germany's most important allies—finally came, it unleashed war on a scale previously undreamed of. After early successes against France and Russia, Germany found itself bogged down in horrific trench warfare in northern France. Each side's fortifications were so powerful that no matter how many men attacked them, they did not fall. Despite this, the generals continued to order assaults, throwing away the lives of an entire generation of young men.

Meanwhile, the Germans continued to acquire a bad reputation based on their methods of fighting. Early in the war, they had invaded neutral Belgium in violation of a treaty, gambling that by doing so they could quickly knock France out of the war. Instead, Britain took the side of France, effectively prolonging the war. Soon the whole world learned stories of German cruelty to the people of occupied Belgium.

Two sailors push a torpedo into the torpedo tube of a U-boat docked in Germany during World War I.

Germany's use of unrestricted submarine warfare (their U-Boats—early submarines— would attack ships without warning) eventually brought the United States into the war on the side of the Allies (France, Britain, Japan, and other countries that were fighting against the Germans). In the end, the Germans lost the war and were forced to sign the humiliating Treaty of Versailles.

The Treaty of Versailles

Signed by a civilian government that had forced the emperor to give up his throne in the last days of the war, the Treaty of Versailles was an extremely bitter blow to Germany. It forced the German people to accept responsibility for the war, and it included a demand for an absurdly high payment of reparations (money given to the Allies as a penalty for starting the war). Alsace-Lorraine was given back to France, and the land between the Rhine River and the French border, known as the Rhineland, was demilitarized—that is, the Germans could not place an army there to defend their borders. Parts of eastern Germany were taken away to create the new nation of Poland. The Germans were forbidden to have an air force, build submarines, or maintain an army larger than 100,000 men. Germany was to be effectively destroyed as a world power.

Many Germans, who had suffered through deprivation and sometimes near-starvation as a result of a British blockade of the country, could not accept these terms. Army veterans felt that the military had been betrayed by the civilian authorities, even though the army had actually collapsed at the very end and their own generals had pleaded with the civilians to negotiate a peace settlement. The blow to German pride was almost impossible to take.

Speer shared these feelings, even though his family had done better than most during the war, and—thanks to his father's sale of land in return for American dollars—continued to thrive in the chaos after the war. Young Albert had played soldier on occasion during the war, even sleeping on the floor of his bedroom for several nights in a row in order to share the discomfort of soldiers in the trenches. But for the most part, he continued with an ordinary childhood. Only thirteen years old when the war ended, he could not understand how, as a German, he was supposed to be responsible for starting World War I, or why he should remain responsible for it his entire life.

A Promising Start

Speer was a sickly child. He suffered from circulatory problems, and probably had very low blood pressure, which made him weak. Worse, he was subject to pains, both real and imaginary, in times of extreme stress. To compensate for this, he worked hard at becoming an outdoorsman, eventually becoming an excellent skier and hiker. He also enjoyed driving cars—his family always managed to have a car, which was a sign of wealth in the years that followed the war. Although very intelligent, he was a lazy student; only in his last years of the German equivalent of high school did he apply himself to getting good grades.

Speer, although friendly and generous, especially with his money, was also rather distant and hard to get to know. He had only a very few close friends and he married the only girlfriend he ever had.

Her name was Margrete Weber, although Speer called her by her nickname, Gretel. She was the daughter of a skilled cabinetmaker, whose extremely close family must have been very inviting to Speer, contrasting as it did with his own cold family life. Considering the Webers to be beneath them, Speer's parents did not approve of Gretel. Both families tried to separate the young pair by sending them to different schools. However, Albert and Gretel continued to write to each other even during their separation, and to see each other during frequent camping holidays, which were popular with German youths of the day.

Meanwhile, Speer was beginning his college education. Although he was very fond of mathematics, his father insisted that Albert follow in his footsteps and train to become an architect. Speer entered a technical school in the southern German city of Karlsruhe in 1923. He studied there for a year and then moved on to a school in Munich, the capital of the German state of Bavaria. There, he met the man who was to be his closest friend for most of his life, a fellow architectural student named Rudolf Wolters.

In 1925, both Wolters and Speer moved on to a school in Berlin, Germany's capital. German architecture was undergoing a revolution during this period, and new schools, such as the Bauhaus style of architects like Walter Gropius, would influence architects around the world for years to come. Yet Speer ended up studying under Heinrich Tessenow, a professor and decidedly average architect who would become the greatest influence in Speer's early life.

Speer himself was not a particularly gifted student—he had trouble making good drawings of his work and frequently he paid others to do them for him—but he was intelligent and organized and he made a strong impression on his professor. Speer graduated in 1928 with a diploma in engineering and stayed on as Tessenow's academic assistant. That year he married Gretel, informing their families that they had done so with a brief telegram.

Speer seemed ready to embark on a new career in architecture just as Germany recovered at last from the effects of the war. With a new bride and a new job, Speer's future seemed to be exceptionally bright. But history was to intervene in his future, in the person of the man who may be responsible for more horrific events of the twentieth century than any other man in history: Adolf Hitler.

2. Hitler's Architect

Adolf Hitler was one of the most influential and murderous people in modern history. Under his direction, Germany—a nation renowned for its music, philosophy, and culture—turned down a deadly path to war, brutality, and genocide. Hitler's depraved personal beliefs became magnified into a sort of national hysteria that touched the life of each and every German. Yet there is a mystery in how a man of modest birth and accomplishments could ensnare so many intelligent people in the web of his own magnetic personality and make them follow his destructive lead.

Hitler was born near Linz, a city in what was then Austria-Hungary, in 1889. In his early years, he had wanted to become an artist or an architect, going so far as to move to Vienna, the capital of Austria, to try to attend school there. He was not accepted, however, and he lived in poverty on the streets of the city, making do by painting picture postcards for tourists.

When World War I started, Hitler enlisted in the German army, rather than the Austrian army. He served as a messenger on the western front, delivering orders to the trenches while under fire from the enemy. He twice received the Iron Cross for his bravery.

Hitler seems to have developed his extreme hatred of the Jews—anti-Semitism—from an early age. His experiences in Vienna, where he met large numbers of Jewish people for the first time, only sharpened these beliefs. After the war, he was one of the many bitter veterans who believed in the betrayal theory; in Hitler's case, however, he felt that the Jews were behind this "betrayal" of the army.

The Nazi Party

After the war, the army assigned Hitler the job of gathering intelligence on the many extremist groups that had formed in Bavaria. He attended a meeting of one of these, called the German Workers' Party, and he was invited to join them after he gave a brief but impassioned speech. He resigned from the army and took over the small party, which he renamed the National Socialist German Workers' Party (usually known by its German initials, NSDAP)—the Nazis.

At this time, many Germans were joining similar organizations (known as *Freikorps*) that opposed the government and were frequently racist and anti-Semitic. Germany's new government, called the Weimar Republic after the city of Weimar in central Germany, where its constitution had been written, was the first truly democratic government in the country's history. However, the government was weakened not only by the terms of the

Versailles treaty but by the discontent of many of its citizens. Both left-wing Communists and right-wing groups like the Freikorps called for a revolution. The economy was in terrible shape, not only because of the effects of the war, but because of the heavy reparations demanded by the Allies. There were fears that the army itself would not be loyal to the democratically elected government.

The Nazis quickly grew into a substantial movement under Hitler's direction. He organized a special section, the *Sturmabteilung* (SA), usually known as the storm troopers or Brownshirts (from the color of the uniforms they wore), composed of common thugs and street criminals. Their job was to beat the opposition—literally—into submission. Hitler attracted veterans, including Hermann Göring, the German fighter ace, to the cause. In 1923, he judged that the time had come to act, and he led the famous failure known as the Beer Hall Putsch.

Putsch is a German word meaning "coup" or "revolution," but Hitler's was more a comedy of errors.

His idea was to enter one of Munich's large beer halls during a rally at which the heads of the Bavarian government were speaking. With his storm troopers he would seize these men, call for the formation of a new government, and then march on Berlin, replacing the Weimar

Members of the feared SA mobilized during the Beer Hall Putsch, which ultimately failed.

government with a new, Nazi organization. He would then go on to tear up the Versailles treaty, build a new army, and seize back the land taken from Germany after the war. He had previously stated his intention to exterminate the Jews. Hitler would eventually succeed in carrying out this program—but not as a result of his Beer Hall Putsch.

Although he managed to capture the leaders of the Bavarian government, the rest of Hitler's plan resulted in disaster. During the night, the government heads managed to slip away from their captors. They ordered the army and the police to crack down on the rebellious Nazis.

Hitler had been convinced that neither the army nor the police would fire on fellow Germans. However, the next day he found out how wrong he was. When the Nazis marched on the center of Munich, the police met them and opened fire. Sixteen Nazis were killed and many were wounded. Hitler fled unharmed but was quickly arrested.

Hitler and Göring (circled) at a march
commemorating the Beer Hall Putsch.

A sympathetic judge sentenced him to only five years for the crime of treason. He ended up serving just nine months of his sentence, using the time to write down his beliefs in his book *Mein Kampf* (My Struggle).

Albert Speer and the Nazis

A student in Munich at the time, Speer seems to have taken no notice of these important events; at any rate, he did not bother to write about it in his letters to Gretel.

The unresolved question of whether he noticed or sympathized with the Nazis is important because it highlights one of the personality traits Speer claimed to have, one that would eventually spare his life at the Nuremberg trial: his ability to show no interest in anything but his work—not to care (to be apolitical) about political affairs.

Hitler had decided on a new tactic after his release from prison in 1924; from that point on, the Nazis would take over the government from the inside by using elections to secure their own power. The party gained membership in every part of Germany, despite the relative health of the German economy, which steadily improved until the disastrous crash of the New York Stock Exchange in 1929 set off a worldwide depression. The government became unstable and was forced

Many German businesses failed and were forced to close during the Great Depression.

to rule by decree, rather than by relying on the Reichstag (Germany's parliament, roughly equivalent to the U.S. Congress), in 1930. That year marked a turning point in Speer's life, for in December he attended a Nazi rally where Hitler himself spoke. Soon after, Speer joined the Nazi Party.

Speer's decision to become a Nazi seems to have been based on what attracted so many other Germans: Hitler's own personal magnetism as a public speaker and the promises he made to restore Germany's former greatness. By this point, vicious and bloody street fighting between the Communists and the Nazis was a common event in Berlin and other cities. Hitler pledged to bring together the German people and end the divisive conflict between the various groups that were trying to lead Germany.

As far as Hitler's views on the Jews and other races, Speer maintained that he ignored them, concentrating instead on Hitler's national policies. At Nuremberg, he repeatedly claimed

Hitler's promises to restore Germany's greatness
drew Speer to the Nazi Party.

ignorance of Hitler's attempts to destroy the Jews in Germany and occupied Europe. As we shall see, however, Speer likely knew more than he said he did at his trial. We must regard his "disinterest" in Hitler's more perverted policies with some suspicion.

Speer enthusiastically threw himself into party life. He joined several Nazi organizations, including the "fighting group" of architects and engineers. Since he had a car, he also joined the NSKK, the *Nationalsozialistisches Kraftfahrkorps*, a sort of carpool for Nazi leaders. It was his job to help drive Nazi officials to and from rallies and meetings.

Meanwhile, the depression had devastated the German economy. Work was extremely hard to find and Speer struggled to get jobs as an architect, once even considering taking a job in Afghanistan. His income from teaching was extremely small and he and Gretel struggled to make ends meet. He did, however, receive one important job (though he was not paid for it): the refurbishing of the headquarters of his *Gauleiter* (the Nazi term for a district party leader), Karl Hanke. Hanke would become an important early contact for Speer within the Nazi leadership.

In 1932, after he was informed that he must accept another pay cut, Speer quit his job as Tessenow's assistant. He and Gretel briefly moved back to his hometown of Mannheim but soon returned to Berlin. That year, Speer met Hitler for the first time, when he had to drive the party head from the airport to a rally. He also received another important commission from Hanke, this time to redecorate the new Nazi headquarters in Berlin, the Adolf Hitler House. Hitler himself was pleased with the young architect's work.

Despite losing the presidential election in 1932 to Germany's former military commander-in-chief, Paul von Hindenburg, the Nazis had made impressive gains. They were now the largest party in the Reichstag, and the Weimar Republic was drowning in chaos. Working behind the scenes with other

right-wing parties (who hoped to dominate
Hitler by bringing him to power under their
terms), the Nazis convinced President
Hindenburg to appoint Hitler chancellor of
Germany on January 20, 1933. His revolution
finally achieved, Hitler quickly moved to
destroy the opposition and cement his hold
on power. In February, Nazi agents set the
Reichstag building on fire and blamed the
Communists; Hitler used this as an excuse
for seizing "emergency powers" that
amounted to making him a dictator. Hitler
had been underestimated, and not for the
last time. Using his new powers, he quickly
destroyed any traces of democracy in
Germany. From then on, his word was law.

Redesigning Germany

Speer, the loyal and devoted party member,
was rewarded now that the Nazis were in
power. He soon was hired to refurbish the
headquarters of the new propaganda

ministry, which was headed by Dr. Joseph Goebbels. Short and thin, with a limp from a club foot, Goebbels was a master at manipulating the emotions of the German people. Although he appeared to have been dissatisfied with Speer's work (he later had the ministry building redecorated), Goebbels became an important ally of Speer's and helped to get him other jobs.

One of these was Speer's stunning design for a rally held at Tempelhof Airport in Berlin on May Day 1933. The young architect hit upon the idea of having a background framed by two huge German flags and the Nazi banner (a red flag with a black swastika in a white circle in the center) brightly lit and contrasting with the darkness of the night. More than 100 spotlights shone directly up in the air, creating a "cathedral of light" ten miles high. The Nazi leadership was highly impressed, and Speer rose in their favor; later that year he was to replicate much of his Berlin rally design for the Nazi Party congress

in Nuremberg. His next major assignment
was to assist Hitler's personal architect, Paul
Troost, in the refurbishment of the
chancellor's apartment in Berlin. At this time,
he began to dine regularly with the Führer (a
German word meaning "leader," and Hitler's
favorite title for himself), developing a
relationship that was as close to friendship as
possible for the two men.

Speer did not waste his newfound access
to Hitler, who had a passion for architecture,
and could recite endless streams of statistics
about his favorite buildings, such as the Paris
Opera. He and Speer shared a taste for the
enormous, for structures that dwarfed the
individual beneath massive stone blocks.
When Troost died in early 1934, Speer filled
the role of Hitler's personal architect.

More and more important commissions
came his way. He designed an enormous
stadium capable of seating 400,000 people
for party rallies in Nuremberg. Soon, he was
put in charge of one of the most audacious

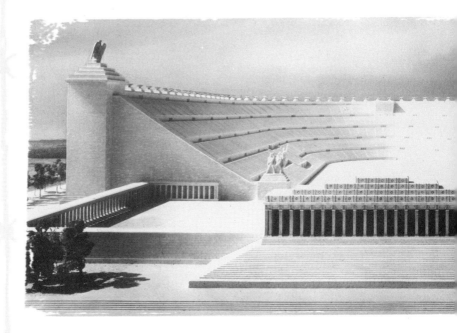

construction plans in history: Hitler's proposed remodeling of Berlin, which would be renamed Germania when completed.

The central feature of Hitler's plan was an enormous boulevard, more than twice as long as Paris's celebrated Champs-Elysées, which would be torn out of the heart of the city. At one end would be a gigantic triumphal arch, almost three times as tall as the Arc de Triomphe in Paris, inscribed with

This is a model of
Albert Speer's design
for a stadium at
Nuremberg to host
the 1938 Olympics.

the names of each of the 1.8 million German soldiers who had died in World War I. At the other end of the boulevard would rise the Great Hall, capped with a huge dome more than 750 feet in diameter and capable of holding more than 150,000 people.

Speer added to the Führer's original designs, placing an enormous reflecting pond to the northwest of the Great Hall, and planning another grand avenue that would run east to west and cross the north-south avenue in front of the Great Hall, creating a "Great Square." Huge public buildings, all designed by Speer, would line these two boulevards. It all was grand on a monstrous scale, coming from the bloated imagination of a man—Hitler—who had to make himself more important than anyone else.

Of course, to achieve this goal, thousands of people living in the center of Berlin would have to be evicted and their homes destroyed. But that mattered little to Hitler. Instead, he made Speer the inspector-general of construction for the Reich capital, or GBI (from the title's initials in German). This position gave Speer the power to destroy buildings, evict people, and demand materials and labor in the German capital.

Speer was also entrusted with the construction of one more major project for Hitler: a new chancellery building that would serve as the official seat of government for Germany. Speer finished the building within a year, a testament to his great ability to organize men, jobs, and materials (an ability that was soon to be of vital importance to Germany).

Speer (at left) shows Hitler his plans for
Berlin's new buildings.

Hitler very much admired the job his architect had done, although the building, only three stories tall, contained much that was tasteless or merely huge for the sake of hugeness. One important feature of the building was a bunker, or fortified hiding place, buried deep beneath it. It was considered necessary in case Berlin was bombed.

Germania was never built. Instead, its planned construction was permanently interrupted by the greatest conflict in human history, a war that would destroy Hitler's Third Reich, and with it most of Speer's great projects, including the chancellery. Berlin would be rebuilt, but only after it had been purged by fire.

3. The World at War

Hitler's ruthlessness was boundless. For example, in 1934 he led a purge of the Nazi Party, ordering the cold-blooded murder of the leadership of the SA, the largest wing of the party. From then on, the leadership of the Party was given to the SS (*Schutzstaffel*, or Protection Squad, also called the Blackshirts because of the color of their uniforms), which had been organized to be loyal only to Hitler. The SS would later run the concentration and forced labor camps, engage in the slaughter of prisoners of war and the enslavement of civilians in the occupied countries, and ultimately preside over the murder of eastern Europe's Jewish population.

Having demonstrated his ruthlessness to his own people, it should not have surprised the world that Hitler would be equally ruthless in his dealings with other nations. Yet from 1936 to 1939, Hitler engineered a series of triumphs that seemed to achieve his dreams of a Greater Germany, one that included all the German-speaking people of Europe.

Step by Step

Hitler's first step, in 1936, was to send troops into the Rhineland, the portion of Germany between the Rhine River and France that the Versailles treaty of World War I had made a demilitarized zone. The tiny German army of 1936 was incapable of resisting the forces of either France or Britain, yet the two western Allies did nothing to prevent the first of many violations of the Versailles treaty. Why? Many governments outside Germany felt that the Treaty of Versailles was too harsh; others feared another senseless slaughter on the scale

German troops march over the Rhine river in Cologne
into the demilitarized zone of the Rhineland,
breaking the terms of the Treaty of Versailles.

of World War I. Still others felt that allowing the Germans to reoccupy the Rhineland would be enough to satisfy Hitler's demands, and that he would ask for nothing else. This policy, which came to be known as appeasement, was to fail time and time again with Hitler.

Hitler increasingly disregarded the Treaty of Versailles. He ordered that the army be

43

expanded, and began creating an air force, the *Luftwaffe.* His next step on the international stage was typically bold: the *Anschluss*— unification with Austria. Like rearmament and occupation of the Rhineland, a partnership with Austria had been forbidden by the Versailles treaty, but Hitler was beyond caring about that. With help from the Germans, Austrian Nazis seized power in their country in 1938, and "invited" the German army to come and restore order. Soon Austria became part of the German Reich.

Hitler's next target was Czechoslovakia. Carved out of the ruins of the Austro-Hungarian Empire at the end of World War I, Czechoslovakia had a substantial German minority inhabiting the region bordering Germany, the Sudetenland. Hitler demanded that the Sudetenland be added to his Germany, because of the "oppression" of the Germans in the region—oppression that did not exist. Because both France and the Soviet Union had treaties with Czechoslovakia, an attempt by

Germany to use force against Czechoslovakia could start a new war in Europe.

Hitler's fellow dictator and ally, Italy's Benito Mussolini, proposed a conference between Britain, France, and Germany. The Czechs were not invited. At this Munich conference, it was decided to give the Sudetenland, with its powerful forts that conceivably could have held off the Germans for some time, to Germany. In return, Hitler promised that this would be his last territorial demand. Not surprisingly, he did not stay true to his word; within a short time the Germans seized the rest of Czechoslovakia, again without opposition from France and Britain.

Blitzkrieg

From the beginning of his rise to power, Hitler had promised to acquire Lebensraum, or "living space," in the east—specifically, Poland and the Soviet Union. In 1939, he took a step toward achieving this dream by negotiating a

Hitler's ally, Italian dictator Benito Mussolini
(left), helped him gain control of Czechoslovakia.

nonaggression pact (an agreement by both sides not to attack one another) with the Soviet Union. As an excuse to take over Poland, he then faked an attack on a German radio station by the Poles. In "response" to the false attack, the German army invaded Poland, which was quickly overrun by the new German tactics of blitzkrieg (German for "lightning war"), which emphasized rapid movement and coordination of tanks and planes. Germany and the Soviet Union divided Poland between them. This time, Britain and France stood by their ally and declared war on Germany. World War II had begun.

Rise to Power

At first, the war had little effect on Albert Speer, who was more concerned with the planned reconstruction of Berlin. Instead of fighting on the front lines, Speer fought the Nazi mayor of Berlin, who resisted Speer's plans for Germania because they would cost the city too much money. Speer, in a remarkable display of his growing talent for working within the Nazi system, outmaneuvered his opponent and managed to have him fired.

Speer was beginning to possess a great deal of power, not only because, as GBI, he could do almost anything he wanted to Berlin, but because of his close access to Hitler. He was

The German invasion devastated Poland.

one of the few regulars at Hitler's mountain resort, Berchtesgarden, in the Bavarian Alps. This access to Hitler meant that Speer could personally put forth his view of things to the Führer, and that he could constantly stay one step ahead of his opponents in the Nazi government. This was very important, because Hitler used a system sometimes called "divide and rule" to manage the Nazis. Important figures in the party were often given broad and overlapping areas to control; this meant that they frequently had disputes with one another, and spent much of their time battling over who should do what. Also, Hitler liked to give out fancy titles to people in the party, who, because of their tremendous egos, were just as eager to accept them. Hermann Göring and Joseph Goebbels were especially famous for their pursuit of more and more empty titles. (Göring, for example, was interior minister of Prussia, plenipotentiary of the four-year plan, head of the Luftwaffe, minister without a portfolio in the German cabinet, and the world's only six-star general.) By keeping his subordinates fighting among each other for greater recognition, and by making sure that each person did not have total control over the area he was assigned to, Hitler very cleverly kept any of the other Nazis from building up a power base with which to challenge him.

In 1940, after several months of inaction that had been dubbed the Phony War by the British and the *Sitzkrieg* ("sitting war") by the Germans, blitzkrieg exploded onto the western front. The Germans stormed through Holland and Belgium, slashing through the Ardennes Forest, which had been presumed by the French to be too rugged for tanks to travel through. The British were surrounded and only managed to escape by means of using every available ship in England to sail their troops out of the city of Dunkirk, on the English Channel.

France surrendered in June 1940, and Hitler made his first and only trip to Paris, the French capital. He brought Speer along to tour the famous Paris Opera with him. Hitler decided not to destroy the beautiful city; instead, he and Speer would outdo it by building Germania.

Speer's power continued to grow as the war dragged on into 1941. The British were alone in standing up to Hitler's plans, resisting a furious effort by the Luftwaffe to knock them out of the war. Speer commanded several "regiments" of skilled construction workers to aid him in the task of rebuilding Berlin according to his plans for Germania. But as the war intensified during 1941, his men were diverted to repair the damage caused by the bombers of Britain's Royal Air Force (RAF). They also constructed bomb shelters, which by August could house about half of Berlin's population. Unlike most of the other senior Nazis, whose departments were usually corrupt and inefficient, Speer showed a talent for streamlining his organization, making it one of the best-run administrations in the Nazi state.

In June 1941, Hitler ordered a sneak attack on the Soviet Union. The move shocked

France surrendered within eight weeks of the Nazi invasion. Hitler and Speer (circled) toured the city in June 1940.

many, even those who had assumed that the two European dictators, Hitler and the Soviet Union's Joseph Stalin, would eventually come to blows. Once again, blitzkrieg seemed unstoppable; the German army steadily advanced eastward, coming close to taking Moscow, the Soviet capital, by the beginning of winter.

But there the German advance stopped. The incredible Russian winter—so cold that soon the only way to start the engines of the German tanks was to light fires beneath them—began to take a cruel toll on the German soldiers, many of whom were still in their thin summer uniforms. The Soviets began to counterattack, using troops equipped for fighting in the winter. By early 1942, it was clear that the first blow had failed to knock the Soviets out of the war; now the Germans would have to fight an enemy with a vastly greater population than their own, one whose factories had been moved out of the range of the German bombers.

Greater Challenges

Early 1942 also brought even greater power to Albert Speer, for in that year he became Reich minister of armaments and munitions, as well as the head of the huge construction network known as the Todt Organization. He succeeded the remarkable Fritz Todt, who had built Germany's network of highways, the Autobahn, as well as many other construction projects. Todt had died in a mysterious plane crash after visiting Hitler. When Speer found out about his death, he expected to be given responsibility for only the construction part of Todt's empire. Instead, he found himself in charge not only of supplying the German armed forces with fuel, planes, guns, tanks, and ammunition, but practically in charge of the entire German economy.

It was a difficult task, but one for which Speer was supremely well suited. He had already shown that he could create and run a highly efficient organization. He was skilled in the game of Nazi politics, and he had a close relationship with Hitler. So even though he had never served in the military or worked in the armaments industry, Speer was an excellent choice to take command of the German economy. However, he faced an enormous challenge. There were many major problems that needed to be solved for Germany to continue fighting.

First, Germany had shortages of many of the raw materials needed to make weapons, tanks, and airplanes. Oil and rubber had to be imported from other countries, as did metals like tungsten and manganese, which were vital for making modern guns and ammunition. The various small countries the Germans had taken over from 1938 to 1942—Austria, Czechoslovakia, Denmark, Belgium, Holland, Norway—helped supply some of these materials, but there were still shortages.

Another problem was the way the German factories were being run. Even in 1942, many factories were not running at full capacity.

Many did not use the efficient assembly-line techniques pioneered by the American Henry Ford, in which each worker had to learn only one small task and repeat it throughout the day. Instead, the German factories often had several people working on a project from start to finish—for example, building an entire airplane over the course of a few days. This meant that each worker had to have a higher level of skill; it also meant that each task took longer to do.

In addition, the United States had entered the war after the Japanese attack on Pearl Harbor on December 7, 1941. Germany had followed their Japanese allies by declaring war on America a few days later. Unlike Hitler and other members of the Nazi leadership, Speer was all too aware of the United States's impressive industrial abilities; already, the Germans were having trouble keeping up with the production of the much smaller Britain. War with both the United States and the Soviet Union would put the German economy under severe strain.

A final problem for Speer was finding enough people to man the armaments factories. Actually, there were two parts to this problem. First, he had to protect the skilled workers who made Germany's weapons from being drafted into the army. He fought a long battle with Hitler and the army commanders to keep these men in their jobs, but with the Soviets attacking in greater numbers, it was hard to keep men inside Germany when they could make a difference on the front lines.

Second, Speer needed unskilled laborers to do much of the work in the factories. There were not enough people in Germany to do this, especially because the Nazis—unlike the British and the Americans—did not like to train women to take over these jobs while the men fought in the war. His solution was to use workers from the countries the Germans were occupying—including slave labor.

The real problem facing Speer was that the Germans were simply unprepared to fight a long war. Hitler's strategy had been based on the overwhelming force of blitzkrieg, which would crush his opponents before they could respond with enough strength to stop him. By using blitzkrieg, he had been able to knock the Poles out of the war in 1939, and then turn around and attack the French in 1940. But the failure to defeat the Soviets quickly in 1941 ruined his plans. The Germans were locked into a two-front war against opponents who vastly outnumbered and outproduced them.

It was a perfect formula for disaster and all that anyone could do was to try and prolong the inevitable. How Speer succeeded in doing just that for so long is one of the most remarkable—and darkest—parts of his life.

4. Inside the Third Reich

Albert Speer now had near-total control over the German war effort. Immediately, he began making reforms to increase its efficiency. He reorganized the various groups that oversaw German industry, making them report directly to him, and cutting away useless jobs and offices. He hired experts to help design new weapons, tanks, and airplanes, as well as to refine the existing designs. Under his guidance, German armament production increased steadily, finally matching that of Britain in 1944.

To make these reforms work, however, Speer was forced to use the power of the Nazi state. He threatened harsh punishments to inefficient managers and anyone else who stood in the way of his success. Most important, his efforts became linked to the central evils of the Nazi state: slave labor and the Holocaust.

Because Speer had so much difficulty finding and keeping enough people to run the German factories, he faced a crucial labor shortage. He attacked these challenges by protecting as many skilled employees as he could, and also by using slave labor to fill in the gaps.

Slave Labor

Slave labor had been a part of the Nazi program ever since Hitler had written *Mein Kampf.* In that book, the soon-to-be Führer had described the future German state in what had been Poland and the Soviet Union as a happy farming community in which the Aryan Germans were a noble class served by their Slavic slaves. German plans for Bohemia and Moravia (once part of Czechoslovakia, and at that time a German "protectorate") were to "Germanize" those who were "racially superior" and kill the rest by either forcing them to do slave labor or sending them to death camps.

Here we must examine Speer's use of slave labor in the German war effort, for this was one of the crimes of which he was eventually convicted at the Nuremberg trials. Speer would save his neck there by two means: by claiming that he never directly ordered slave labor to be used and that he had tried to improve the conditions of the laborers in German factories.

The first part is true, technically speaking: Speer had not issued direct orders for the use of slave labor; indeed, labor was not under the control of his ministry. Instead, he had asked Fritz Sauckel, the commissioner general for labor deployment, to fill the quotas Speer gave him. In other words, Speer would ask Sauckel for a certain number of workers to fill his munitions factories, and

Sauckel would round them up in the occupied countries and deliver them.

However, it is undeniable that Speer used the slaves whenever he could, and he most likely knew of the unsavory methods Sauckel used to force people to work for the Germans. (Sauckel was executed by the Allies at the Nuremberg trials for the crimes he

The Nazis forced many prisoners to work as slaves for the German war effort and for some German companies.

committed in forcing so many people of the occupied nations to work for the Germans.)

From a practical viewpoint, however, Speer realized that forced labor was inefficient. Not only was it difficult to make the captured people work effectively, but the act of forcing people to work for their conquerors made many so mad that they began to actively resist the Nazis. Speer therefore developed schemes to allow the workers in the occupied nations to make war goods other than weapons in their own countries. This plan succeeded much better than rounding up people and shipping them into Germany, and because of it, France, Belgium, and Holland were spared Fritz Sauckel's despicable methods.

This scheme to use foreign workers was one of the points of defense Speer used after the war to deflect charges that he had ordered or even had wanted forced labor; indeed, it would seem to indicate that he considered forced labor inefficient. It was also used as an example of how he had tried to improve the living conditions of the laborers who worked for the German war effort.

However, it seems as though Speer was not motivated by moral concerns about the welfare of the prisoners; rather, his concern was how efficient they could be. Poor living conditions resulted in low productivity, which Speer despised and Germany could not afford. His opinions were based on what he saw during visits to a concentration camp and a forced labor camp. These two visits are important, because they tie into the most controversial question about Speer's life: How much did he know about the Holocaust?

In March of 1943, Speer visited Mauthausen, an SS concentration camp in occupied Czechoslovakia. After touring the facility, he wrote a letter to Heinrich Himmler, the head of the SS and therefore the one in charge of all of Germany's concentration camps, recommending that less "permanent" construction techniques be used in the concentration camps. Speer thought the

Prisoners were forced to build V-2 rockets in the
infamous tunnels of Dora.

existing buildings were excessive and
wasteful, despite the fact that Mauthausen's
own commander admitted that the buildings
and sanitary facilities were so bad that disease
was wiping out the prisoners.

In December 1944, Speer visited Dora, an
authentic forced labor camp, in the Harz
Mountains of central Germany. It was here
that the infamous V-2 rockets were built by

Forced laborers built tail sections for
V-2 rockets.

prisoners taken from the Buchenwald concentration camp. Dora was a terrible place made up of underground tunnels in which its workers labored for eighteen hours a day, sleeping and eating there as well. Only once a week did they come above ground. Sanitation was terrible, and the food was inedible. Half of the workers who came through Camp Dora eventually died.

Speer was horrified by the conditions at Dora, which were so shocking that several members of his staff who had accompanied him to the camp had to go on leave to recover from what they had seen. He immediately ordered changes to be made. The workers were given quarters above ground, as well as more food and medical attention. In the last year of the war, the death rate declined at Camp Dora. However, as Speer testified at the Nuremberg trials, this was done less out of sympathy for the plight of humanity than because he simply needed healthy workers.

Mauthausen and Dora were the only two camps Speer is on record as having visited. Yet his vast munitions empire within the Third Reich embraced the slave labor of all the Reich's prisoners, including those of the Jews in the extermination camps. Despite this, after the war, Speer claimed to have had no direct knowledge of what was happening to the Jewish population of occupied Europe.

The Final Solution

From the start of his political career, Hitler's intentions to destroy all the Jews in Germany had been crystal clear. Since his concept of a Greater Germany would eventually include "living space" carved out of Poland and the Soviet Union, it was obvious that he also intended to exterminate the Jewish communities of those countries. Almost as soon as he had taken power, Hitler had begun to attack the Jews of Germany. A set of restrictive laws, known as the Nuremberg

Laws, stripped Jews of their citizenship and forbade them from marrying Aryans or from hiring non-Jews as servants. These laws had been passed in 1935. The Nazi definition of Jewishness was a racial one and had nothing to do with what religion a person practiced; under the Nuremberg Laws, a person needed to have only one Jewish grandparent to be considered a Jew. Nazi attacks on Jews continued to escalate all through the late 1930s, coming to a bloody climax on November 9, 1938, a night known as *Kristallnacht*, or "The Night of Broken Glass." On this night, the Nazis went on a rampage throughout Germany, smashing the windows of stores owned by Jewish people and attacking and killing Jews in the streets. Millions of dollars of damage was done and the Nazis added insult to injury by requiring the Jews to pay for the damages themselves.

Once the war had started and Poland had come firmly under the heel of the Nazi boot, the full measure of Hitler's hatred was focused on the Jewish people. The SS began to actively exterminate the Jews of Poland and the Soviet Union, and Soviet prisoners of war as well, especially the commissars, Communist Party officials who served with the military units to make sure that they remained loyal to the Communist government of the Soviet Union.

Such officers were shot on sight whenever they were found by the *Einsatzkommando,*

Nazis killed Jews and destroyed Jewish businesses during Kristallnacht on November 9, 1938.

the "Special Action" commandos, squads of SS men who followed the German army to accomplish the grim task set for them by Adolf Hitler. Their name stemmed from the ironically mild expression that the SS hid horrible crimes behind: "special treatment." Special treatment meant hanging, deportation to the camps that sprang up in Poland for the Jews, and shooting. Overall, special treatment meant extermination.

As hardened and unemotional as the *Einsatzkommando* were, even they could not kill as quickly or efficiently as the Nazi leadership desired. On January 20, 1942, in the Berlin suburb of Wannsee, the senior SS leadership met and decided how to carry out the *Endlösung,* or "Final Solution" for the "problem" of Europe's Jews. This was yet another innocent expression for a terrible crime: the Final Solution would be to kill the Jews.

Experiments had already been carried out on the eastern front by the *Einsatzkommando* using "death vans," specially made vans whose passenger compartments were sealed off while exhaust fumes were pumped in, eventually killing the occupants. These had proved efficient—and easier on the nerves of the Nazi death-squad members; at that time, the SS proposed to repeat the process on a larger scale. New labor camps were set up in central Poland for the dual purpose of producing equipment for the war and exterminating their occupants. The largest and most infamous of these was Auschwitz; others were Treblinka, Belzec, Sobibor, and Chelmno.

Throughout Germany and the occupied countries, Jews were rounded up and packed tightly together into cattle cars without food or water, so that many of them died before they could even reach their destination. Once they had arrived in the camp, SS doctors would inspect them; those who were healthy were put to hard labor, clothed insufficiently, and fed just enough to slowly starve. The rest—the sick, the elderly, the children—were sent to the gas chambers.

These chambers were disguised as disinfection rooms. Those who were forced inside were told to take off their clothes and go into a shower room. But instead of water, Zyklon-B, a pesticide, would come hissing out of the shower heads, filling the room with poisonous vapors. The doors to the chamber were airtight and were sealed from the outside, yet the people inside the room tried to force them open. When the chambers were opened, the largest pile of dead bodies would be directly in front of the doors, which were often marked with scratches from the victims' fingernails.

After the procedure had been completed, the bodies were gathered up and stripped of any remaining valuables, including gold dental fillings. Then the corpses were burned in huge ovens, called crematoria. The smoke from the burning bodies constantly hung over the camps, making the air foul with the stench of burning flesh.

This was the Final Solution, the cruel and cold-blooded murder of millions. Yet despite this fantastic effort—the coordinated slaughter of people from all parts of Europe—and the high priority given to this most depraved of Hitler's desires, Albert Speer claimed not to know what was happening. At Nuremberg, his claim of ignorance (coupled with his statement that, even though he did not know what was happening, as a senior member of the Nazi government he must share the guilt

These are the ovens at the Mauthausen concentration camp crematoria, where many Jews were murdered.

for what had occurred) probably saved his life. Speer maintained that he did not know to what extent the Final Solution was being realized, and that he did nothing to help it along. However, evidence that disputed this claim eventually came to light.

Evacuation

As part of his duties as GBI of the reconstruction of Berlin, Speer had to demolish parts of the city; this required him to find housing for the people whose homes were destroyed. Later, of course, it was the Allied bombs that did the demolition, but the problem remained the same: where to put these now-homeless Germans. Under Nazi rule, there was one easy answer: Evict Jews from their homes and put the displaced Germans in them. Over the course of the war, several thousand such apartments were opened up, and their rightful tenants were "evacuated." At this point, evacuation meant being shipped east to the death camps of Poland, but Speer would claim not to know the Jews' ultimate destination.

Not only would Speer claim that he had not known about the fate of his evacuees, but also he attempted to hide the fact that he had evicted Jews from Berlin. The book he wrote about his life, *Inside the Third Reich*, makes no mention of the apartments he seized during the war. Furthermore, the chronicle of his activities as GBI, kept by his good friend and then-employee Rudolf Wolters, was deliberately altered after the war to remove the passages referring to the eviction of the Jews of Berlin. Only the chance survival of a portion of another copy of the chronicle allowed researchers to discover Wolters's forgery. (After Wolters's death, the full, unedited version of the chronicle was donated to the German government archives.)

Speer, then, was at least partially responsible for the deaths of many of Berlin's Jews in the Holocaust. But what of his claim that he did not know about the mass slaughter that was occurring around him? Here, too, Speer may not have told everything he knew. The question seems to be whether he attended a speech by the head of the SS, Heinrich Himmler, in Posen, in occupied Poland, on October 6, 1943.

This much is known: Speer addressed the Gauleiters, the leaders of the Nazi Party districts, in the morning, urging, as he usually did, increased production and total commitment to the war effort. In the afternoon, Himmler spoke and openly described for one of the first times the terrible secret the SS was hiding in Poland: the Final Solution. He spoke of the necessity for keeping it a secret from the German people, and about how hard it was to accomplish the task. In the speech, he apparently addressed Speer directly, as if he were there.

When the details of this speech were brought to light in 1971, Speer immediately denied that he had been there. He claimed that Himmler had simply used a conversational tone in his speech, but that he was not, in fact, speaking directly to a present Speer. Or perhaps Himmler, who was notoriously nearsighted, had simply mistaken someone else for Speer. Later, an old friend of Speer's swore that the two of them had driven away from the conference in Posen just after lunch, meaning that he could not have been present at Himmler's speech.

Although these explanations may sound unconvincing, it is also true that there is no direct evidence that Speer *was* at the Posen conference; therefore, it cannot be proven that he definitely knew about the horrors of the SS extermination camps. Still, Speer was a member of Hitler's inner circle and had frequent contact with Himmler, who by 1944 had confessed to the senior generals of the German army the murders his men were committing in Poland. Therefore, it is unlikely that Speer did not know about the purpose of Auschwitz and the other camps in Poland.

Maintaining the Fighting Machine

Meanwhile, Speer continued his impressive work in maintaining the German war machine. Production continued to steadily increase; if it remained less than that of Britain, his results still were much better than any of the people before him had been able to attain. Speer increased production of tanks and fighter planes, which were vital to the German war effort; he also coordinated the repairs of the factories that were attacked regularly by the Americans and the British, often managing to lose only a few days of production before the damage was repaired. In all, his work was a model of efficiency, with only a few notable exceptions.

One of these exceptions was the jet fighter. The Germans were far more advanced in this area than either the Americans or the British, and they soon had working models of a fighter that was faster than any other combat aircraft of its day. A jet-powered fighter was a near-ideal

plane to defend Germany from enemy
bombers; it was so fast that the guns on the
heavy bombers could not move quickly enough
to shoot at it. However, Hitler was fixated on
attacking at the expense of defense, and he
ordered that the jets be turned into bombers to
carry the war to England. This was a waste of
effort; the planes simply could not carry
enough bombs to do much damage. By the

The Nazis built the first jet aircraft. A German
Messerschmitt ME 110 flies over Poland.

time the jets were once more converted to defense, the Allied bombings had destroyed the factories that made their special fuel.

Another example of this kind of waste was the effort Speer put into the V-2 rocket. This "terror" weapon was designed to attack the British; it could not be intercepted like a bomber (the rockets flew so high they almost left the atmosphere), and, since it traveled faster than sound, it would hit its target before people on the ground could even hear it coming. However, despite the highly advanced technology used in it, the rocket was still extremely inaccurate; worse, it carried a relatively small amount of explosive. In the long run, the Germans would have been better off developing new, heavy bombers instead.

Still, despite these failures, Speer had managed to keep the German army running even as the Allies began to close in on Germany. But the Third Reich's days were numbered; soon, it was to collapse utterly, leaving Speer to face the victorious Allies alone.

5. Defeat and Victory

In 1942, the Germans launched a second invasion of the Soviet Union, this time targeting the oil fields of the Caucasus region in the south. Once again, the Soviets attacked, and they managed to surround the German Sixth Army in the city of Stalingrad. Hitler refused to allow the army to retreat and after several weeks of vicious, house-to-house fighting, the exhausted and starving Germans surrendered on February 2, 1943. For the Germans, it was the turning point of the war; they would be in constant retreat from this point on.

In December 1943, Speer went on a trip to the occupied regions of Norway, Finland, and Russia to inspect the army bases and other facilities there. He and his staff treated it like an enormous camping trip, hiking and skiing cross-country. After sleeping outside one night, Speer developed shooting pains in his left knee. By the time he had returned to Germany, the knee had swollen up. Speer was forced to take time off and go into the hospital.

Although the cause of his painful knee was only an infection, he developed a serious medical problem while in the hospital—a blood clot in his lung nearly killed him. His recovery was long and slow; he left Germany to rest in a castle in the Italian Alps, where he remained until April 1944.

Speer's illness had a serious effect on him. For the first time since he had become a part of Hitler's inner circle, he lost faith in the Führer. Although he remained loyal to Hitler and continued to do impressive work in keeping Germany in the war, some of Hitler's magical hold on him had been broken. This would have important consequences both for Speer and for Germany.

The Fall

The war was increasing in intensity by 1944. On June 6, the Americans and British had landed on the beaches of Normandy, in northern France, and their combined armies swept through France and on toward the Rhine. Meanwhile, the long-awaited Soviet invasion of eastern Europe had begun, with the Soviet Red Army sweeping aside the Germans as they drove toward Berlin. It soon became clear to rational observers that Germany could not hope to hold the territory it had conquered. Rational observers, however, were in short supply in the Nazi state, and were soon to become even more rare.

On July 20, 1944, a group of high-ranking army officers and other Germans tried to assassinate Hitler. A briefcase containing a bomb was placed inside his conference room during a strategy meeting. Four men died from the blast, although Hitler was shielded by a heavy conference table, and was spared. The

On June 6, 1944, American and British troops
stormed the beaches of Normandy, France.

conspirators had planned to seize Berlin once
the Führer was dead, but when news of his
survival reached the capital, the revolution—
and the last chance to end the war without an
invasion of Germany—fizzled out. Speer had
not been part of the conspiracy, although his
name appeared with a question mark after it
on a list of possible members of the new
government the conspirators hoped to create.

In a sense, this confirmed Speer's own view of himself: an apolitical public servant, dedicated only to the task he had been given.

Speer continued in this role, helping to supply the German army for its last-ditch effort to defeat the Allies, the Battle of the Bulge, in December 1944. After its failure, he had to confront the terrifying disaster into which Hitler was then threatening to plunge all of Germany.

Convinced that after his death the German people should not survive, Hitler issued orders to destroy all the bridges, factories, power plants, and roads of Germany to prevent their use by the invading Allies. This would bring nothing but horror and misery to the German people, but Hitler had never considered their suffering before.

Speer opposed Hitler's "scorched earth" policy. By arguing and pleading with Hitler, he managed to prevent these orders from being carried out until the very last days of the war.

During the winter of 1945, Speer even gave thought to assassinating Hitler himself. He later claimed that he managed to acquire a poison gas bomb, which he intended to drop into the ventilation system of Hitler's bunker beneath his own chancellery building. His attempt was foiled, he said, by SS guards and a special shield that had been placed on the ventilation system. Researchers have since noted that Speer himself had designed the ventilation system to resist just such an attack, so his claims of an assassination attempt seem questionable.

Adolf Hitler committed suicide on April 30, 1945, making Grand Admiral Karl Dönitz head of the government in his will. Speer had joined the admiral in northern Germany shortly before that. He remained a part of the German "government" even after Germany's unconditional surrender on May 7, 1945. He was interrogated by the Americans, who were interested in finding out how effective their bombings had been, especially since the Japanese were still fighting in the Pacific. Then, on May 23, 1945, Speer was arrested by the

British. The time had come for Speer to face punishment for what he had done.

Taking Responsibility

The International Military Tribunal had been established by the British, French, Americans, and Soviets to prosecute the Nazi leadership for "crimes against humanity."

Speer (in tan coat) and other Nazi officials are seen here shortly after their arrests.

These included starting wars in violation of international treaties, as well as the abuse of human rights that had taken place in Germany and in the Nazi-occupied countries during the war. Although conducted like a trial, it was understood from the start that certain of the defendants were going to be judged guilty. The only question for many of them was what the punishment would be.

Speer had been one of the most cooperative of the senior German prisoners. Unlike the bullying Hermann Göring, the highest-ranking of the Nazi prisoners, Speer gladly gave information to his captors, and he refused to work with Göring in presenting a unified defense. This was for a very simple reason: Unlike the Reich marshall, Speer had a good chance of avoiding the death penalty.

Speer certainly was not guilty of the main crimes of the Nazi state. He had not been involved in the planning for the invasions of the surrounding countries. He had not organized the awful machinery of the Final

Solution, whatever he had done indirectly to support it. In the absence of the evidence of the chronicle kept by Rudolf Wolters (believed to be lost) or the minutes of the Posen meeting, Speer could believably claim to have no knowledge of the Holocaust. More important, he made a crucial and dangerous choice: He would accept some of the blame

Speer (circled) and other high-ranking Nazi officials await their fates at the Nuremberg trials.

for crimes of the Nazi regime. During his testimony, although not admitting to any specific crime, he said that as a member of the Nazi government he had to be judged as responsible, in some measure, for its crimes.

Albert Speer was the only one of the prisoners to accept any guilt for what had happened. This, taken with his work to prevent the scorched earth policy (an example of his resistance of Hitler's orders) and his claim to have tried to assassinate the Nazi leader, saved his life. While Göring and others were sentenced to hang, Speer escaped with only a twenty-year prison sentence. He had won perhaps the greatest victory of his life, and had escaped the total destruction and defeat of the Nazi empire.

6. A Mystery

Albert Speer spent the next twenty years of his life in Spandau Prison, in West Berlin, along with seven other high-ranking Nazis. No other prisoners were held in Spandau. The seven Nazis were guarded by French, British, American, and Soviet soldiers. Toward the end of his sentence, Speer shared the prison only with Rudolf Hess, once deputy Führer to Hitler himself, whose mental health had been getting steadily worse ever since his mad solo flight to Britain in 1941,which apparently was taken in a misguided attempt to meet with Churchill and open up peace talks.

A prison can take an enormous physical and mental toll on those who are held within its walls, and the lives of the Nazi prisoners were

This is the exterior of Spandau Prison, where Speer and other Nazi war criminals were incarcerated.

deliberately made difficult. They were extremely restricted in the number of letters they could exchange with people from the outside world. Visits with family members were also extremely restricted. Every attempt was made to silently bury the prisoners within the walls of Spandau.

Despite this, Speer survived his experience remarkably well. This was due in no small part to the elaborate network of secret messages smuggled in and out of the prison, which was coordinated by his close friend, Rudolf Wolters. Speer also adopted his own peculiar methods for keeping his sanity. He planted a formal garden in the prison recreation yard and measured its dimensions by pacing them out. By keeping track of how many times he had walked around the yard, he measured how far he had traveled. By the end of his prison stay, he had walked over two-thirds the distance around the globe.

Speer was released in 1965, and he made a painful transition to civilian life. His children were almost all grown then; he moved in with Gretel in the house in Heidelberg that he had grown up hating. He began the last phase of his career: apologizing for the Nazi regime, and for his own part in it.

He had already begun work on his memoirs while in Spandau, writing his thoughts down on scraps of paper and smuggling them out to friends and relatives. He finished them after

Speer (center) and his wife are surrounded by reporters after his release from Spandau Prison.

his release from Spandau and they were published in 1969 as *Inside the Third Reich.* The public, fascinated by the first close look at Hitler by a man who had been his friend, snatched the book up and made it a bestseller. Speer would follow this book with another about his life in prison, *Spandau: The Secret Diaries,* which was published in 1976, and a third book, *Infiltration,* about way the SS and the Nazis took over the German state, which was published after his death in 1981. In these books, Speer continued the defense he had begun at Nuremberg: apologizing for the evil of the Nazi state and taking the blame for its atrocities, but refusing to admit any personal guilt.

Toward the end of his life, as we have seen, this stance became controversial. The discovery that the chronicle of his activities in the Nazi government had been tampered with was a serious blow to his credibility, especially when it became clear that some of the passages described how he had helped evict Berlin's Jews, sending them to almost certain death in the concentration camps. The revelation that he may have been at Himmler's Posen speech also made his claim of ignorance of the Holocaust seem like a convenient lie. These were both serious charges, for it still was possible that he could be tried by the German government for war crimes, even after his release from Spandau.

After his release from prison, Albert Speer poses
with plans for Hitler's palace.

Speer's ugly past threw a long shadow over
the last years of his life, which came to an end
on August 31, 1981. He died of a stroke while
in England to tape a television interview.

In the end, Albert Speer will always remain
a mystery to us. He was a man who could
block everything out of his mind but the job
at hand: In a regime dedicated to one of the
most evil ideologies of the twentieth century,
he managed to remain largely apolitical,
working only to do the best job that he could.

Yet by doing so, he helped the Third Reich
wage the most destructive war in history for
much longer than it might otherwise have
lasted. And, although he showed courage and
remorse by accepting his guilt in being a part
of this monstrous government, he hid within
his confession a lie about his own personal
part in the enormous tragedy that Hitler
wrought upon Germany and the world, a lie
which threatened to undo him until the end
of his life.

Speer's lack of interest in politics helped to mask his own enormous ego—which was transformed into gigantic public monuments of stone and steel—and his basic ruthlessness, a drive to get to the top no matter what. It was these qualities that lay behind his Nuremberg defense, and it is because of them that we cannot in the end accept his claim to be the one "good" Nazi.

Timeline

March 19, 1905	Berthold Konrad Hermann Albert Speer is born in Mannheim, in southern Germany.
1919	Treaty of Versailles is signed; assigns blame for World War I to Germany.
1928	Speer marries Margrete "Gretel" Weber.
1930	Speer joins the Nazi Party.
1932	Speer meets Hitler for the first time.
1933	Hitler becomes chancellor of Germany and assumes dictatorial powers.

Speer begins work refurbishing and designing Nazi buildings. |
| **1934** | Speer becomes Hitler's architect and begins plans to build Germania. |

1938	Nazis seize power in Austria, making it part of the German Reich.
	Kristallnacht, the Night of Broken Glass.
1939	Germany invades Poland; World War II begins.
1940	Blitzkrieg expands to the west.
1941	Hitler attempts to conquer the Soviet Union.
	The United States enters World War II on the side of the Allies.
1942	Speer becomes Reich minister of armaments and munitions, and head of the Todt Organization.
	The senior SS leadership meets to strategize the Final Solution.
1943	Speer visits the SS concentration camp Mauthausen.
	Heinrich Himmler's speech at Posen.
1944	Speer visits Dora, the forced-labor camp whose inhumane conditions appalled him.

1944   Under Speer's direction, German
                            armament production finally
                            matches Britain's.

                            German army officers attempt to
                            assassinate Hitler.

                            Germany's last chance to defeat
                            the Allies, the Battle of the Bulge,
                            ends in failure.

1945   Hitler commits suicide;
                            Germany surrenders.

May 23, 1945   Speer arrested by the British; at the
                            Nuremberg trials, the International
                            Tribunal of War Crimes sentences
                            Speer to twenty years in prison.

August 31, 1981   Speer dies of a stroke while
                            visiting England.

Glossary

Allies
The nations, including Britain, France, the Soviet
   Union, and the United States, that fought against
   Germany and its allies during World War II.

Anschluss
German for "unification"; refers to the unification
   of Austria and Germany that was specifically
   forbidden by the Treaty of Versailles.

anti-Semitism
Discrimination against Jews.

apolitical
Having no interest in politics.

appeasement
To pacify an aggressor by giving in to his or
   her demands.

Auschwitz
The largest and most infamous of the German

extermination camps in Poland; located near
the town of Oswiecim in central Poland.

blitzkrieg
German for "lightning war"; refers to the
combined air and tank attacks perfected by the
Germans during World War II.

crematoria
Huge ovens used to burn bodies of gas
chamber victims.

Einsatzkommando
"Special Action Commandos," the killing
squads organized by the SS to exterminate
Jews and others in the conquered regions of
eastern Europe.

Final Solution (Endlösung)
The Nazi plan to exterminate the Jews of Europe.

Führer
German word for "leader"; Hitler's title while he
was dictator of Germany.

genocide
The systematic and planned extermination of an
entire national, racial, political, or ethnic group.

Germania
The planned name for Hitler's remodeled Berlin.

Kristallnacht

"The Night of Broken Glass," November 9, 1938, when the Nazis rampaged throughout Germany, destroying Jewish businesses and synagogues.

Luftwaffe

The German air force in World War II.

Nazism (National Socialism)

The theories of the Nazi Party as dictated by Adolf Hitler.

NSDAP

The German initials for the National Socialist German Workers' Party, the official name of the Nazi Party.

SA (Sturmabteilung)

The storm troopers, or Brownshirts; a collection of thugs and criminals that was the original enforcement branch of the Nazi Party until replaced by the SS.

SS (Schutzstaffel)

The black-uniformed elite of the Nazi Party, which controlled the Gestapo and ran the concentration and extermination camps.

Treaty of Versailles

Treaty that ended World War I and imposed harsh terms on Gemany.

For More Information

American-Israeli Cooperative Enterprise (AICE)
2810 Blaine Drive
Chevy Chase, MD 20815
(301) 565-3918
Web site: http://www.us-israel.org

Anti-Defamation League
823 United Nations Plaza
New York, NY 10017
(212) 490-2525
Web site: http://www.adl.org

Simon Wiesenthal Center
1399 South Roxbury
Los Angeles, CA 90035
(800) 900-9036
(310) 553-9036
Web site: http://www.wiesenthal.com

United States Holocaust Memorial Museum
100 Raoul Wallenberg Place SW
Washington, DC 20024-2126
(202) 488-6100
Web site: http://www.ushmm.org

Web Sites

History Place
http://www.historyplace.com

The Holocaust History Project
http://www.holocaust-history.org

Museum of Tolerance
http://www.wiesenthal.com/mot

Remember.org: Cybrary of the Holocaust
http://www.remember.org

Who's Who in Nazi Germany
http://www.thomson.com/routledge/who/
    germany/intro.html

For Further Reading

Adler, David A. *We Remember the Holocaust.* New York: Henry Holt, 1995.

Ayer, Eleanor H. *The United States Holocaust Memorial Museum: America Keeps the Memory Alive.* New York: Dillon Press, 1994.

Chaikin, Miriam. *A Nightmare in History: The Holocaust, 1933–1945.* New York: Clarion Books, 1987.

Fox, Anne L., and Eva Abraham-Podietz. *Ten Thousand Children: True Stories Told by Children Who Escaped the Holocaust on the Kindertransport.* West Orange, NJ: Behrman House, 1998.

Frank, Anne. *Diary of a Young Girl: The Definitive Edition.* New York: Bantam Books, 1997.

Kallen, Stuart A. *The Nazis Seize Power, 1933–1941: Jewish Life Before the Holocaust.* Edina, MN: Abdo Publishing Co., 1994.

Rice Jr., Earle. *Nazi War Criminals.* San Diego: Lucent Books, 1997.

For Further Reading

Rochman, Hazel, and Darlene Z. McCampbell, eds. *Bearing Witness: Stories of the Holocaust.* New York: Orchard Books, 1995.

Wiesel, Elie. *Night.* New York: Bantam Books, 1982.

For Advanced Readers:

Gilbert, Martin. *The Holocaust: A History of the Jews of Europe During the Second World War.* New York: Henry Holt, 1987.

Sereny, Gitta. *Albert Speer: His Battle With Truth.* New York: Vintage, 1996.

Shirer, William L. *The Rise and Fall of the Third Reich.* New York: MJF Books, 1998.

Speer, Albert. *Inside the Third Reich.* New York: Touchstone Books, 1997.

Speer, Albert. *Spandau: The Secret Diaries.* London: Phoenix Press, 2000.

Spiegelman, Art. *Maus: A Survivor's Tale: My Father Bleeds History.* New York: Pantheon, 1997.

Spiegelman, Art. *Maus II: A Survivor's Tale. And Here My Troubles Began.* New York: Pantheon Books, 1992.

Van der Vat, Dan. *The Good Nazi: The Life and Lies of Albert Speer.* New York: Houghton Mifflin, 1997.

Index

Credits

About the Author
Fred Ramen is a writer and computer programmer who lives in New York City.

Photo Credits
Cover © Ullstein Bild; p. 11 © Michael Maslan Historic Photographs/Corbis; p. 13 © Corbis; p. 24 © Roland Klemig, courtesy of USHMM Photo Archives; p. 26 © Mary Evans Picture Library; pp. 28 and 52 © Bildarchiv Preussischer Kulturbesitz, Berlin, 2001; p. 30 © AP Wide World; p. 36 and 37 © Stadtarchiv Nuernberg, courtesy of USHMM; pp. 39, 80, 88, 90, 93 © Hulton Getty/Archive Photos; p. 43 © Hulton Getty/Liaison Agency; p. 46 © Muzej Revolucije Narodnosti Jugoslavije, courtesy of USHMM; p. 48 © Bundesarchiv; p. 62 © Main Commission for the Prosecution of the Crimes against the Polish Nation, courtesy of USHMM; pp. 65, 66 © Ullstein Bild; pp. 70 and 85 © National Archives, courtesy of USHMM; p. 74 © Marie Ellifritz, courtesy of USHMM; p. 95 © Deutsche Presse/Archive Photos; p. 97 © Superstock.

Series Design
Cynthia Williamson